DONALD TRUMP

By Bray Jacobson

BOTH SIDES of the Aisle

Enslow PUBLISHING

I0806975

Please visit our website, www.enslow.com. For a free color catalog of all our high-quality books, call toll free 1-800-398-2504 or fax 1-877-980-4454.

Library of Congress Cataloging-in-Publication Data

Names: Jacobson, Bray author
Title: Donald Trump / Bray Jacobson.
Description: Buffalo, New York : Enslow Publishing, [2026] | Series: Both sides of the aisle | Includes bibliographical references and index.
Identifiers: LCCN 2025023740 (print) | LCCN 2025023741 (ebook) | ISBN 9781978546608 library binding | ISBN 9781978546592 paperback | ISBN 9781978546615 ebook
Subjects: LCSH: Trump, Donald, 1946—Juvenile literature | Presidents–United States–Biography–Juvenile literature | Businessmen–United States–Biography–Juvenile literature | United States–Politics and government–2017-2021–Juvenile literature | United States–Politics and government–2021—Juvenile literature | LCGFT: Biographies
Classification: LCC E913 .J33 2026 (print) | LCC E913 (ebook) | DDC 973.935–dc23/eng/20250825
LC record available at https://lccn.loc.gov/2025023740
LC ebook record available at https://lccn.loc.gov/2025023741

Published in 2026 by
Enslow Publishing
2544 Clinton Street
Buffalo, NY 14224

Copyright © 2026 Enslow Publishing

Portions of this work were originally authored by Ryan Nagelhout and published as *Before Donald Trump Was President*. All new material in this edition is authored by Bray Jacobson.

Designer: Andrea Davison-Bartolotta
Editor: Therese Shea

Photo credits: Cover, p. 1 (main) noamgalai/Shutterstock.com; cover, p. 1 (buildings) Fandorina Liza/Shutterstock.com; series art (background stars) v_kulieva/Shutterstock.com; series art (watercolor background) Apostrophe/Shutterstock.com; p. 5 Joshua Sukoff/Shutterstock.com; p. 7 Seth Poppel/Yearbook Library/File:Donald Trump NYMA (colorized).jpg_commons.wikimedia.org; p. 9 Gotfryd, Bernard/Donald Trump with Fred Trump_loc.com; p. 11 John Penney/Shutterstock.com, (inset) Wangkun Jia/Shutterstock.com; p. 12 sweeann/Shutterstock.com; p. 13 Evan El-Amin/Shutterstock.com, (inset) Harrison Ha/Shutterstock.com; p. 14 Debby Wong/Shutterstock.com; p. 15 Jay Dixit/File:Sebastian Stan at "The Apprentice" in NYC 03.jpg_commons.wikimedia.org, (inset) carrie-nelson/Shutterstock.com; p. 17 Matt Smith Photographer/Shutterstock.com; p. 19 Philip Yabut/Shutterstock.com

Some of the images in this book illustrate individuals who are models. The depictions do not imply actual situations or events.

All rights reserved. No part of this book may be reproduced in any form without permission in writing from the publisher, except by a reviewer.

Printed in the United States of America
CPSIA compliance information: Batch #CWENS26: For further information contact Enslow Publishing, at 1-800-398-2504.

Find us on

CONTENTS

Words in the glossary appear in **bold** type the first time they are used in the text.

THE 47TH PRESIDENT

On January 20, 2025, Donald Trump became U.S. president for the second time. In his inaugural address, or first speech, he said:

> *If we work together, there is nothing we cannot do and no dream we cannot achieve. Many people thought it was impossible for me to stage such a historic political comeback. But as you see today, here I am. The American people have spoken.*

To many, Trump is a **controversial** president. Others find hope in his promise of American success at home and around the world.

MORE TO **KNOW**

Political means having to do with politics, or the activities of the government and government officials.

While at a rally in Pennsylvania in July 2024, someone shot at Trump. His ear was hit, but he was otherwise unharmed. One man at the rally was killed, however.

GROWING UP TRUMP

Donald John Trump's birthday is June 14, 1946. He was born in Queens, New York, to Frederick and Mary MacLeod Trump. He grew up with two brothers, Fred Jr. and Robert, and two sisters, Elizabeth and Maryanne.

Donald's family had a lot of money. His father worked in real estate, or the buying and selling of property. Fred Trump built and owned apartments in Queens, Staten Island, and Brooklyn in New York City. At one time, Fred Trump was worth more than $200 million!

MORE TO KNOW

Trump was high-spirited as a child and was sent to the New York Military Academy when he was 13. His parents hoped he would learn **discipline** there.

Trump graduated, or finished classes, from the military academy in 1964.

FAMILY BUSINESS

Trump went to college at Fordham University in New York City for two years. Then, he went to the Wharton School at the University of Pennsylvania. Trump graduated in 1968 with a degree in **economics**.

While he was in school, Trump worked for his father's real estate business, Elizabeth Trump & Son. After he graduated, he joined the business full-time. In 1971, he was given control of the company, which he renamed the Trump Organization.

MORE TO KNOW

While at Wharton, Trump bought property in Philadelphia, Pennsylvania, where the school is located.

Donald Trump is shown here as a young businessman with his father Fred.

NEW YORK AND BEYOND

As Trump opened hotels and buildings around New York City, he became well-known around the country. He named many of his projects after himself, including Trump Plaza. One of Trump's most famous buildings opened in New York City in 1983—the 58-story Trump Tower.

Trump's business grew to include properties all around the world. Trump's hotels can be found in many major cities, including Chicago, Illinois; Las Vegas, Nevada; Miami, Florida; and Dubai, United Arab Emirates.

MORE TO KNOW

Trump and other members of his family have lived at Trump Tower since it was built in the 1980s.

The Trump Organization has also built golf courses all around the United States and in other countries such as Scotland, the United Arab Emirates, and Ireland.

ALL IN THE FAMILY

Trump has five children. He married his first wife, Ivana Zelníčková, in 1977. Together, they had two sons, Donald Jr. and Eric, and a daughter, Ivanka. Trump had another daughter, Tiffany, with his second wife, Marla Maples. In 2005, Trump married his third wife, Melania Knauss. They had a son, Barron, a year later.

Trump has worked with his adult children at times. Donald Jr., Eric, and Ivanka have played big roles at the Trump Organization.

In 1987, Trump cowrote a book called *Trump: The Art of the Deal*. It includes business advice as well as stories from Trump's life.

MORE TO **KNOW**

As of 2025, Donald Trump has 11 grandchildren.

ERIC, IVANKA, AND DON JR.

THE APPRENTICE

America learned more about Trump and his business through a "reality competition" show. This is a kind of TV show where real people are filmed as they try to win a game. The show was called *The Apprentice*.

On the show, businesspeople worked to finish tasks and **impress** Trump. The person who did the worst would be "fired" by Trump. The person who did the best might be hired. The show ran as *The Apprentice* for six seasons. It became *The Celebrity Apprentice* for eight more seasons.

THE CELEBRITY APPRENTICE

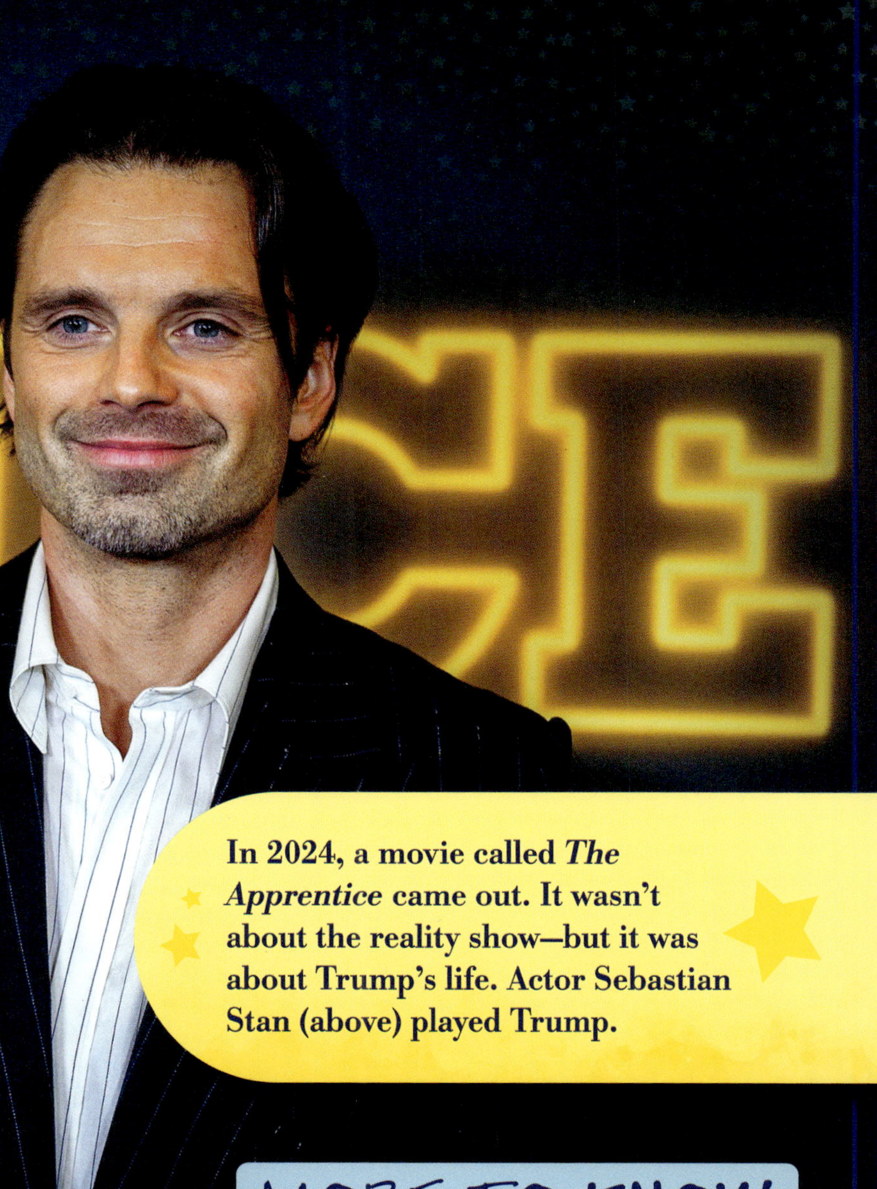

In 2024, a movie called *The Apprentice* came out. It wasn't about the reality show—but it was about Trump's life. Actor Sebastian Stan (above) played Trump.

MORE TO KNOW

Trump has a star on the Hollywood Walk of Fame.

TO THE WHITE HOUSE

Over the years, Trump thought about running for president of the United States. In 2015, he announced he was finally going to do it. Trump beat out 16 other Republicans to win the party's **nomination**.

Trump stirred national pride and promised more jobs. He was **elected** the 45th U.S. president in November 2016. During his term in office, Trump nominated three justices to the Supreme Court, the highest court in the United States. He worked to better the tax code. However, he was also **impeached** in 2019.

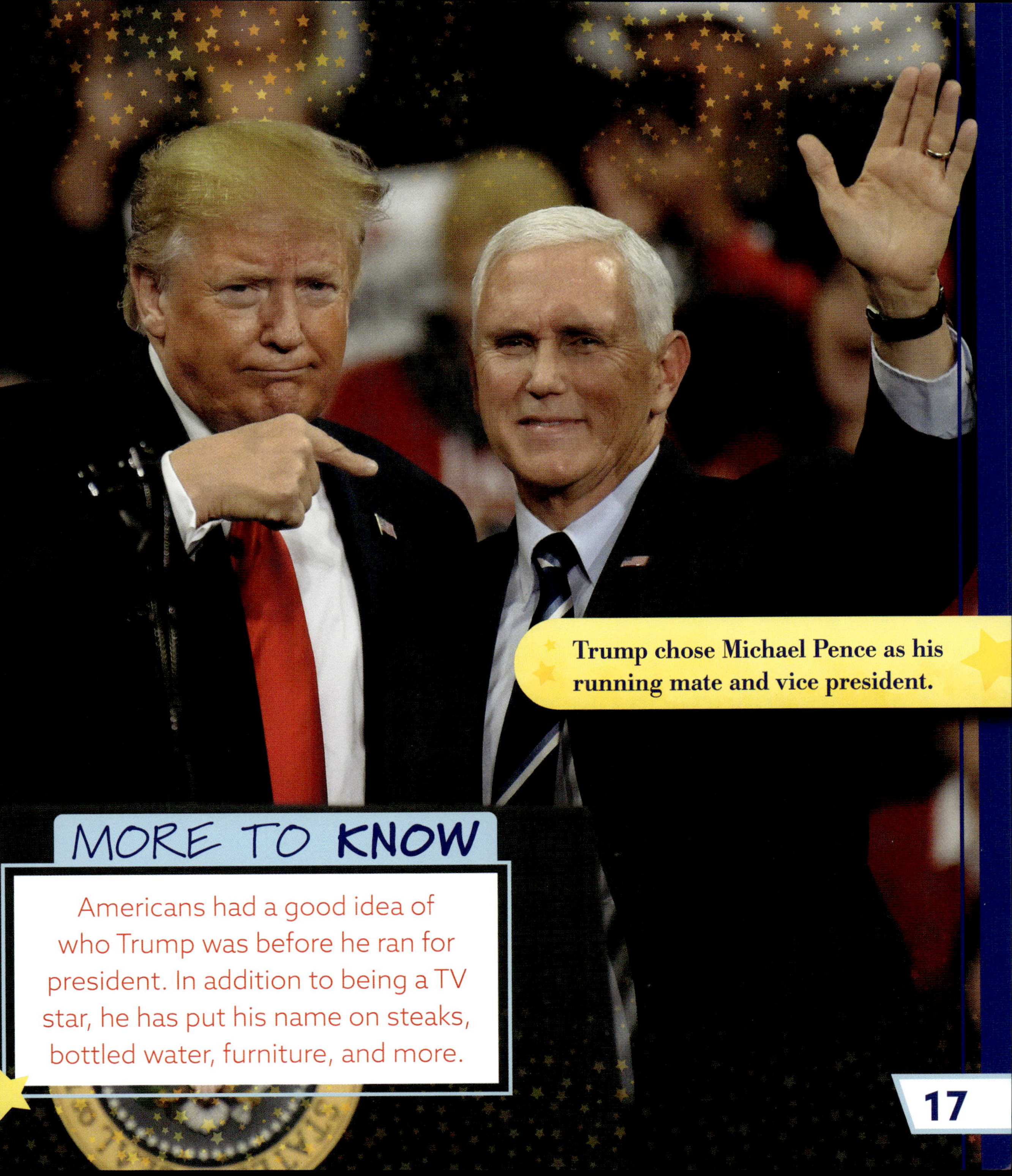

Trump chose Michael Pence as his running mate and vice president.

MORE TO KNOW

Americans had a good idea of who Trump was before he ran for president. In addition to being a TV star, he has put his name on steaks, bottled water, furniture, and more.

JANUARY 6TH

Trump ran for reelection in 2020. Joe Biden, a long-time member of Congress and former vice president, won the presidency. Trump and his supporters were not happy with this outcome.

On January 6, 2021, Trump held a rally in Washington, DC. In his speech, he said the election had been stolen from him. He encouraged his supporters to fight against the **certification** of the election results. A crowd went on to attack the U.S. Capitol. More than 100 police officers were hurt in the **riot**.

MORE TO **KNOW**

The January 6th attack on the Capitol is sometimes called an insurrection. An insurrection is an act of **revolt** against a government.

Trump's second impeachment in 2021 happened because of the January 6 attack. Some people in Congress believed his speech caused the people to riot.

BACK IN THE WHITE HOUSE

Trump again earned the Republican nomination for president in 2024. In the November 2024 election, he defeated Democratic nominee Kamala Harris.

During the first 100 days of Trump's second term, he used executive orders and actions to show the power of the presidency. He **focused** on **immigration** problems, high government spending, and trade with other countries, among other issues.

Trump's presidency will no doubt continue to have a big impact on the United States and Americans for years to come.

MORE TO KNOW

An executive order is a piece of writing signed by the president that tells the U.S. government to do something. Executive actions include executive orders as well as other directions from the president.

Trump's Timeline

1946	Donald John Trump is born on June 14.
1959	He begins attending New York Military Academy.
1968	He graduates from the Wharton School at the University of Pennsylvania.
1971	He takes over his father's business and renames it the Trump Organization.
1987	*Trump: The Art of the Deal* comes out.
2004	*The Apprentice* first airs.
2016	Trump wins the presidential election.
2017	He is sworn in as the 45th president on January 20.
2020	He loses the presidential election.
2021	The January 6th riot and attack on the U.S. Capitol occurs.
2024	Trump wins the presidential election.
2025	He is sworn in as the 47th president on January 20.

In 2024, Trump won votes in states he had lost in the 2020 election.

GLOSSARY

certification: The act of making something official.

controversial: Something many people disagree about.

discipline: A type of conduct that includes following rules and practicing self-control.

economics: The study of how goods and services are made and used.

elect: To choose for a position in a government.

focus: To direct your attention or effort to something specific.

immigration: The process of coming to a country to settle there.

impeach: To charge with misconduct in office.

impress: To gain another's interest.

nomination: The act of choosing someone to run for office.

revolt: An uprising against an established authority.

riot: A public disturbance during which a group of angry people become noisy and out of control.

FOR MORE INFORMATION

Books

Fleischer, Jeff. *Votes of Confidence: A Young Person's Guide to American Elections*. Minneapolis, MN: Zest Books, 2024.

Hansen, Grace. *Donald Trump: 45th and 47th President of the United States of America*. Minneapolis, MN: Abdo Kids, 2025.

Our Country's Presidents: A Complete Encyclopedia of the U.S. Presidency. Washington, DC: National Geographic, 2025.

Websites

President Donald J. Trump
www.whitehouse.gov/administration/donald-j-trump/
Read more about Donald Trump on the White House website.

The Presidents
www.whitehousehistory.org/collections/president-biographies
Read more about all U.S. presidents in history here.

Publisher's note to educators and parents: Our editors have carefully reviewed these websites to ensure that they are suitable for students. Many websites change frequently, however, and we cannot guarantee that a site's future contents will continue to meet our high standards of quality and educational value. Be advised that students should be closely supervised whenever they access the internet.

INDEX